GLEN URQUHART SCHOOL
74 Hart Street
Beverly Farms, MA 01915

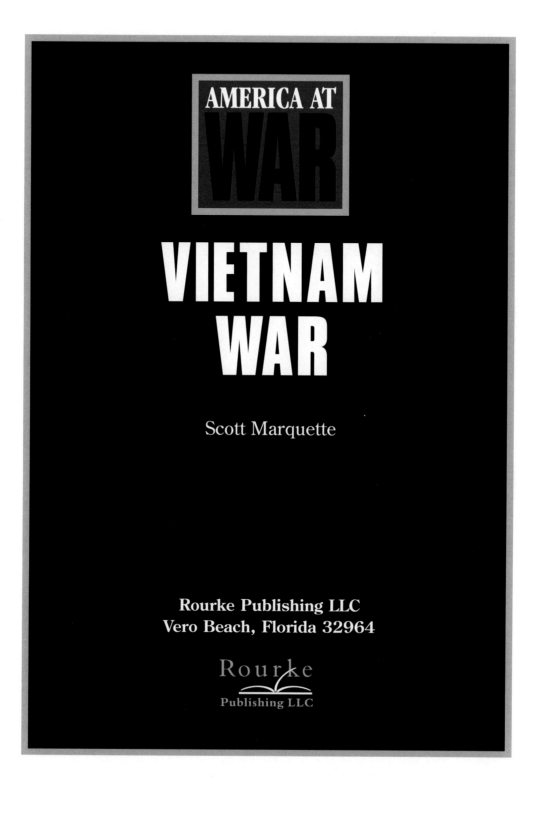

AMERICA AT WAR

VIETNAM WAR

Scott Marquette

Rourke Publishing LLC
Vero Beach, Florida 32964

Rourke
Publishing LLC

PHOTO CREDITS:
U.S. Army Center of Military History: cover, page 8; National Archives and Records Administration: pages 4, 26, 30, 32; Defense Visual Information Center: pages 6, 10, 16, 20, 23, 35, 38; AP/Wide World Photo: pages 12, 14, 18, 28, 36, 42; Lyndon Baines Johnson Library and Museum: page 24; Getty Images: page 40; Corbis Images: page 44.

PRODUCED by Lownik Communication Services, Inc. www.lcs-impact.com
DESIGNED by Cunningham Design

Library of Congress Cataloging-in-Publication Data

Marquette, Scott.
  Vietnam War / Scott Marquette.
    p. cm. — (America at war)
  Summary: Traces the history of the unpopular war that killed over 58,000 Americans, discussing the causes and effects, leaders, major battles, guerrilla warfare, aerial bombing, weaponry, peace negotiations, and lessons learned.
Includes bibliographical references and index.
  ISBN 1-58952-391-1 (hardcover)
  1. Vietnamese Conflict, 1961-1975—Juvenile literature.
  [1. Vietnamese Conflict, 1961-1975.] I. Title. II. Series.

DS557.7 .M358 2002
959.70404'3—dc21   2002001219

Printed in the USA

Cover Photo:
A helicopter brings supplies to Army infantry troops in the jungles of Vietnam.

Table of Contents

The Vietnam War was the most controversial in American history. At the war's height, most Americans thought it was a mistake.

Introduction

The War We Lost

For many Americans, the war in Vietnam is a bad memory. It was the most unpopular war in our history. At home, the U.S. was split in two, as protests against the war turned angry and sometimes violent. It led to the downfall of one president and helped bring down another.

Millions of Vietnamese and 58,000 Americans lost their lives in a distant war few people understood. For the thousands of families who had to flee their homes in Vietnam and come to the U.S., the war brings memories of horror and loss.

But for many Americans, Vietnam is a bad memory because it is the war we lost. In other wars, the U.S. did not always achieve all of the things it wanted. But in Vietnam, we failed at the one thing we most wanted to do. We could not keep Vietnam from becoming a communist country.

Today, Americans still talk about the Vietnam War. It still has its effect on our lives, on our government, and on how we think about the world. Most of all, the war we lost changed the way we look at war itself.

*Thousands of Americans were killed or wounded in the war,
which spread from Vietnam into Laos and Cambodia.*

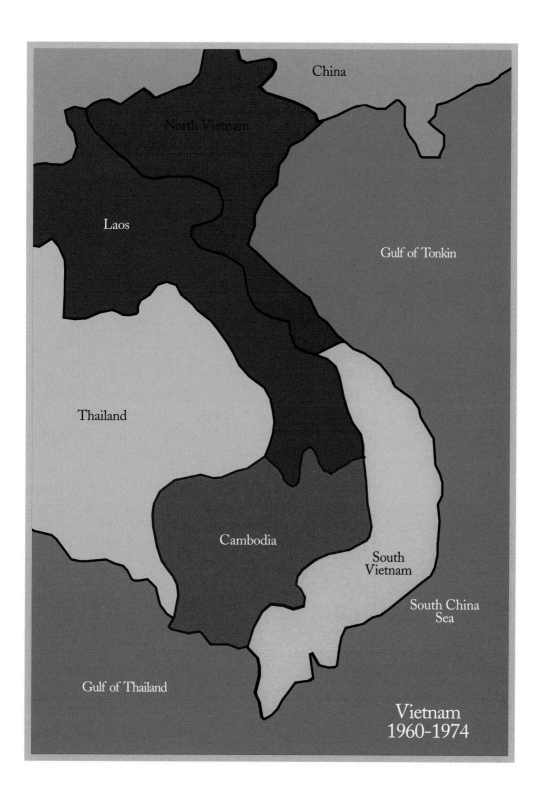

China

North Vietnam

Laos

Gulf of Tonkin

Thailand

Cambodia

South
Vietnam

South China
Sea

Gulf of Thailand

Vietnam
1960-1974

7

VIETNAM WAR TIMELINE

1945
September 2: Ho Chi Minh declares Vietnam to be an independent republic

1954
July 21: France and Vietnam sign agreement to temporarily split Vietnam into north and south

1955
Ngo Dinh Diem declares S. Vietnam to be the Republic of Vietnam

1963
August 4: Congress passes Gulf of Tonkin Resolution

1965
October: Battle of Ia Drang Valley

1967
December: Siege of Khe Sahn begins

1968
January: North Vietnam launches the Tet Offensive

May 13: Paris Peace Talks begin

1969
March: President Nixon begins secret bombing of Cambodia

1970
April: U.S. troops invade Cambodia

May 4: Four student protesters killed at Kent State University

1973
January 27: All parties sign the Treaty of Paris

March 29: Last U.S. troops leave Vietnam

1975
January 7: North Vietnam launches massive attack on the south

April 30: South Vietnam surrenders

Hearts and Minds

From the late 1800s until 1939, Vietnam was ruled by France. But in 1940, Japan invaded the country. A group called the **Viet Minh** fought their country's invaders. Their leader, **Ho Chi Minh**, wanted Vietnam to be a free country. He wanted the Japanese to leave, but he did not want the French to come back. The U.S. helped the Viet Minh fight the Japanese.

World War II ended and the Japanese left in 1945. Ho declared Vietnam to be a **democratic republic**. But France did not want to lose Vietnam. They sent in troops and drove the Viet Minh to the north of the country.

Ho asked the U.S. to support Vietnam's independence. But the U.S. had changed its mind about the Viet Minh. America was

Ho Chi Minh

Ho Chi Minh was the son of an official in the court of the Vietnamese emperor.
As a young man, he took a job as a cook on a French ship. He spent time in the U.S., England, France, China, and the Soviet Union before coming back to his home to fight Japan.

In the Vietnam war, the U.S. was unable to prevent communists from the north from taking over the entire country.

now in a **Cold War** with communist countries like the Soviet Union and China. The U.S. feared that Vietnam would fall to the communists. If that happened, the U.S. thought more countries in Asia would turn communist, too. People thought of the countries falling one by one. They feared it would be like a row of dominoes falling over. This idea was called the **Domino Theory**.

To stop communist rule, the U.S. supported the French against the Viet Minh. But the war did not go well for France. After losing major battles, the French called for a peace treaty. Under the treaty, the French troops would move to the south, while the Viet Minh stayed in the north. The people of Vietnam would then vote for the leaders they wanted and the French would leave.

The U.S. did not support the treaty. Instead, the U.S. picked a leader to rule the southern part of the country. He was **Ngo Dinh Diem**. Diem would not hold an election for the whole country. In 1954, he declared that the southern half of the country would be a new nation, called the Republic of Vietnam.

Viet Minh fighters who lived in the south joined other people who did not like the Diem government and formed a new group. It was called the National

In World War II, Ho Chi Minh helped the Allies fight the Japanese in Vietnam. After the war, he wanted Vietnam to be a democratic republic.

Liberation Front (or NLF). North Vietnam supported the NLF. Diem called these fighters that opposed him the **Viet Cong**.

Diem's army could not defeat the NLF. He asked the U.S. for help. At first, the U.S. sent only a few men. But by 1963 there were almost 17,000 U.S. troops in Vietnam. The U.S. also sent ships and planes to support Diem.

In August 1964, two U.S. warships said gunboats from North Vietnam had fired on them. President Lyndon Johnson asked Congress for more power to fight the war. Congress did not declare war on Vietnam. Instead, they passed an act that let Johnson use more force against North Vietnam. The act was called the **Gulf of Tonkin Resolution**, after the waters where the U.S. ships said they were when shots were fired at them. America was about to step up its role in the Vietnam War.

U.S. troops were not used to fighting the kind of guerrilla war they faced in the jungles of Vietnam.

Search and Destroy

U.S. forces in Vietnam grew fast after the Gulf of Tonkin Resolution. In March 1965, 3,500 Marines landed. By June, 74,000 U.S. troops were in the country.

This was not the kind of war that the U.S. was used to fighting. There were no enemy lines to attack. Instead, NLF forces were all around them. They often lived in the villages U.S. troops were supposed to protect. They hid in tunnels and in the jungle. And there was no land to capture. The NLF troops would simply leave or hide when U.S. forces came and return when the Americans went away. This kind of fighting is called a **guerrilla war**.

The leader of the U.S. troops, General William Westmoreland, wanted a new plan for fighting the NLF. Instead of attacking enemy lines or trying to capture their land, the U.S. would just try to kill as many of their men as it could. U.S. troops would destroy their stores of weapons and food. Westmoreland thought the NLF would get tired of fighting and give up. His plan was called a **war of attrition**.

To weaken the NLF, U.S. troops went on **search and destroy** missions. Patrols would go to villages and look for NLF fighters and supplies. Sometimes

The Americans relied on helicopters to help them move quickly above the dangerous jungles and swampy rice paddies of Vietnam.

they would burn the whole village if they thought it was an enemy base.

In October 1965, the North Vietnamese Army (or NVA) tried to drive the U.S. out of the **Ia Drang Valley** in central Vietnam. The U.S. Army faced waves of NVA soldiers for a month. But the U.S. won the battle, killing many NVA forces. The Battle of Ia Drang was one of the largest battles of the war. It taught the NLF and NVA not to fight long battles against U.S. soldiers. Instead, they would attack quickly and pull back just as fast.

Westmoreland and Johnson were pleased with how the war was going. So many NVA and NLF troops were being killed they thought the war would soon be over. But the NVA and NLF were stronger than the U.S. thought. In 1967, they planned an attack to prove they were not near defeat.

In December, North Vietnamese troops moved in

Life of a "Grunt"

U.S. infantry soldiers in Vietnam called themselves "grunts." Fighting in the jungles was a dangerous job. They had to move through dense forests and swamps in very hot weather. Soldiers were killed by hidden traps made from sharpened bamboo poles. Unseen enemies in the jungle often shot at them.

North Vietnamese troops charge during the siege of the Marine base at Khe Sahn.

around the Marine base at **Khe Sahn**. They fired thousands of **artillery** shells into the base. They shot down planes and helicopters that tried to land. In the hills, 20,000 NVA troops waited to storm Khe Sahn when supplies ran out.

But Westmoreland ordered that Khe Sahn be held at all costs. To support the base, 50,000 Marines and U.S. Army troops were sent in. They fired back at the NVA artillery and called in planes to bomb the NVA positions. The battle continued for 77 terrible days. In the end, the U.S. held the base. More than 250 Americans had lost their lives. But more than 1,600 NVA troops had been killed. It looked like a major win for the U.S.

The United States dropped tons of bombs on North Vietnamese targets in its war of attrition against communist forces.

Quagmire

Even though the U.S. thought it was winning the war in Vietnam, it had to send more and more men to fight. As many as half a million U.S. troops were in the country at the peak of the war. This made some Americans wonder whether the U.S. really was winning. They feared we were getting bogged down in the war. They called Vietnam a **quagmire**— a swamp that was hard to get out of.

U.S. planes bombed targets in both North Vietnam and South Vietnam. The U.S. flew as many as 150,000 bombing runs each year. The bombs were meant to destroy NVA and NLF troops and bases. But it was often hard to tell which towns were real targets. Many innocent people were killed in the bombing.

U.S. officials told Americans back home that the communists were being driven out of the south. But in early 1968, the NLF launched a new attack that shocked the U.S. Their attack came on **Tet**, the Vietnamese new year. More than 85,000 NLF troops stormed every large city in the south, all at once. They attacked **Saigon**, the capital of South Vietnam, and took the U.S. Embassy. They held it for eight hours. It took the U.S. three weeks to drive the NLF

Lyndon Johnson

Lyndon Johnson became president in 1963 after President John F. Kennedy was killed. At the same time he was fighting the war in Vietnam, he also called for a "War on Poverty" in the U.S. He started many new programs to help the poor. But spending on both "wars" caused a big government debt.

back out of the capital city.

The bloodiest fight took place in the country's old capital, **Hue**. Marines had to go from house to house, looking for NLF and NVA troops that were waiting to kill them off. Both sides fired artillery into the city. The shells killed civilians and destroyed homes. The city was destroyed. More than 100,000 people who lived there were left homeless.

The attack, called the **Tet Offensive**, lasted until the fall. It was not a military win for the north. About 45,000 NVA and NLF soldiers died. But the huge fight came at a time when President Johnson said that communist forces were almost wiped out. This made people feel they could not trust the president. It made the war even less popular at home.

In 1968, Johnson felt he could not win another

The surprise NVA and NLF attack during the Tet Offensive showed that America's enemies were not about to surrender.

President Lyndon Johnson lost popular support for his leadership of the war. In 1968 he announced he would not run for another term.

term as president. He announced he would not run again. The new president, Richard Nixon, said he had a new plan to end the war. He would pull troops out of Vietnam. At the same time, he would step up the bombing, especially in the north. He hoped that this would force North Vietnam to agree to a peace treaty. He said his plan would bring "peace with honor."

*Young people across America
protested against the war in Vietnam.*

The War at Home

At first, many Americans were in favor of the war in Vietnam. They did not want to see Asia turn communist. But as the war went on, many people changed their minds.

One thing that caused people to question the war was the **draft**. To get enough men to fight the war, the U.S. called young men to join the military, whether they wanted to or not. This turned young people against the war. Some of them left the country to avoid the draft. Others went to jail because they did not believe in the war. College students could get out of the draft. People thought it was not fair to poor men who could not go to college.

Many of the men drafted were African Americans. Some thought the draft was **racist**. **Civil rights** leaders like Martin Luther King, Jr. and Malcolm X called for the U.S. to end the war. People at home grieved for all the U.S. troops killed in the war. They did not like the fact that so many civilians were killed by U.S. bombs. They did not trust what the government told them about the war. By the end of the 1960s, more than half of all Americans felt the war was wrong.

Four students were killed when National Guard troops tried to stop protests at Kent State University.

Students and other people gathered in public to protest the war. In November 1969, 40,000 of them went to Washington, D.C. to call for an end to the war. At times, the protests turned into riots. Protesters fought with police who tried to stop them.

The worst time came on May 4, 1970, at a protest at Kent State University in Ohio. National Guard troops were called out to stop a riot. The troops panicked and shot at the crowd. The shots killed four students and hurt eleven more. The sight of students killed by U.S. troops turned many people against the war.

The war had other effects on life at home. By 1967, the U.S. was spending $2 billion a month on the war. The U.S. tried to pay for the war by raising taxes and printing more money. This caused **inflation**. Prices

Peaceniks and Hippies

When the war was still supported at home, people called student protesters peaceniks. But soon many young people did more than just oppose the war. They questioned the whole American way of life. They became hippies. They dropped out of society, wore long hair and wild clothes, and took drugs.

In November, 1969, 40,000 students went to Washington, D.C. to call for the end of the war. These students protested outside the Pentagon.

went up faster and faster. Growing prices and higher taxes hit Americans hard.

The growing feeling against the war had forced President Johnson out of office. When President Nixon's new plan did not bring peace soon, he lost support, too. Americans were angry at their leaders and angry at each other. Some people feared the country would come apart.

*In January 1973,
representatives of the U.S. and North and South Vietnam
signed a peace treaty in Paris.*

"Peace with Honor"

President Johnson had started peace talks with North Vietnam in Paris. It was just after the start of the Tet Offensive. But the talks did not go far. South Vietnam's new president, **Nguyen Van Thieu**, said he would not make peace with communists.

When Nixon became president in 1969, he kept the talks going. But neither side could agree on a plan for peace. North Vietnam wanted the U.S. to leave. They wanted the NLF to have a role in a new government. The U.S. wanted all enemy troops to be pulled out of the south. With the talks stalled, Nixon decided to put more pressure on the north.

North Vietnam moved troops and supplies to the south through **Cambodia** and **Laos**, the lands to the west. Nixon decided to bomb enemy supply lines in Cambodia. In April 1970, Nixon sent U.S. troops into the country. The next year, troops from South Vietnam—backed up by U.S. planes—entered Laos. The spread of the war brought new protests in the U.S. But Nixon said the moves would help end the war.

A large NVA force crossed into the south and attacked the South Vietnamese troops in March 1972. The attack was called the **Easter Offensive**.

The NVA easily beat the southern troops, but Nixon ordered heavy bombing of the area. He also bombed the north's capital, **Hanoi**. The bombing crushed the NVA attack and killed 100,000 troops. In the face of the loss, North Vietnam came back to the peace talks in Paris.

Napalm and Agent Orange

The U.S. used new weapons to fight in the jungles of Vietnam. Napalm was a kind of jellied gasoline. Dropped from planes, it burned everything in its path. Agent Orange was a spray that killed plants so the enemy could not hide in the brush.

Nixon had his own reasons for wanting the war to end soon. The heavy bombing, and the war in Laos and Cambodia, had made many Americans angry. In 1973, Congress said it would cut all funds for the war and try to remove Nixon from office. Nixon ordered all fighting in Vietnam stopped early that year.

In January, all sides signed a treaty to end the war. The U.S. would leave Vietnam. A cease-fire would end fighting between North and South. The two sides would work to form a new government.

The last U.S. troops left Vietnam in March 1973.

*Despite the peace treaty, South Vietnamese troops
continued to attack enemy towns.*

Panicked South Vietnamese troops continued to attack enemy towns.

But the cease-fire did not last long. Thieu sent his troops to attack enemy towns. But without U.S. support, his rule began to break down. North Vietnam launched a major attack in 1975 and quickly defeated the southern troops. Thieu fled the country. On April 30, South Vietnam gave up. Vietnam was now one country. It was under communist rule.

Even though Ho Chi Minh died in 1969, his dream for a Vietnam free of foreign rule had come true. But for the U.S., the fall of South Vietnam was a bitter defeat.

The Vietnam Veterans' Memorial features the names of Americans who died in the war.

The Lessons of Vietnam

The Vietnam war had a huge effect, both on the U.S. and on Vietnam. More than 58,000 U.S. soldiers died. Many of those who came back suffered from wounds or mental illness. Most felt they got a poor welcome from a country that did not like the war they fought.

Vietnam took decades to recover from the loss of life and damage of the war. Almost 30 years later, it is still trying to rebuild. Many Vietnamese fled the country, often in small boats. Some came to live in the U.S.

In Cambodia, the war led to the fall of the government. The new

General William Westmoreland

William Westmoreland led troops in World War II and Korea before being named head of U.S. troops in Vietnam. At first he was popular in the U.S. *Time* magazine even named him Man of the Year in 1965. But after the shock of the Tet Offensive, Lyndon Johnson replaced him.

Today, Vietnam is beginning to build a thriving economy.
But it is still under communist rule.

rulers were the **Khmer Rouge**. They put millions of their own people to death.

The huge cost of the war led to more inflation and budget shortfalls. These problems would plague the U.S. until the 1990s. Richard Nixon lost more support when men who worked for him were caught breaking into Democratic Party offices. This break-in became known as Watergate. Nixon had to resign in 1974.

For years after the end of the war, people talked about what America should have learned from it. They talked about the "Lessons of Vietnam." But people did not agree on what those lessons were supposed to be.

Some thought the lesson was that all war is wrong. They thought we should look for new ways to solve our problems with other countries. Others thought the lesson was that we should not fight in guerrilla wars where it was not clear who we were fighting. And some thought we should not fight a war unless we were sure we were going to win.

After Vietnam, people in the U.S. did not feel the same about war. They were less willing to support a war. It was almost 10 years before the U.S. used its troops once more in a foreign land. The Vietnam War comes up each time we think about sending men to fight. When troops went to Afghanistan in

Secretary of State Colin Powell visited Vietnam in 2001.
The U.S. is forming closer ties to its old enemy.

2001, some feared it might be "another Vietnam."

Even in the 21st century, Vietnam still has an impact. People who run for president often must tell what they did during the war years. Were they for the war or against it? Did they fight in Vietnam or find ways to get out of fighting?

Today, Vietnam is still ruled by communists. But its leaders have begun to give people more freedom. They have more say in how they want to live. For decades, the U.S. would not trade with Vietnam. But it went back to full relations with its old enemy in 1995.

In 1982, the Vietnam Veterans' Memorial was built in Washington, D.C. Its black stone walls show the names of Americans killed in the war. Some did not like the design of the monument. Soon, though, people started to flock to it. Millions still go there each year. They mourn the dead and think of the lessons of Vietnam.

Thirty years later, Americans are still trying to learn the lessons of Vietnam.

Further Reading

Devaney, John. *The Vietnam War.* Franklin Watts, 1993.

Kilborne, Sarah S. *Leaving Vietnam: The Journey of Tuan Ngo, a Boat Boy.* Simon & Schuster, 1999.

Myers, Walter Dean. *A Place Called Heartbreak: A Story of Vietnam.* Steck-Vaughn, 1993.

Sevastiades, Patra McSharry. *The Vietnam Veterans Memorial.* Rosen, 1997.

Zeinert, Karen. *The Valiant Women of the Vietnam War.* Millbrook Press, 2000.

Websites to Visit
Battlefield: Vietnam
www.pbs.org/battlefieldvietnam

Vietnam: A Television History
www.pbs.org/wgbh/amex/vietnam

The Vietnam War Resource Guide
http://members.aol.com/veterans/warlib6v.htm/

Glossary

artillery — large guns that fire explosive shells

Cambodia — country in southeast Asia invaded during the Vietnam war

civil rights — the movement to gain equal rights for African Americans

Cold War — conflict between the United States and the Soviet Union between 1945 and 1990

democratic republic — a country where the people elect their leaders

Domino Theory — the belief that if one country fell to communism, its neighbors would soon fall, too

draft — a law that requires people to serve in the armed forces if needed

Easter Offensive — the 1972 attack by NVA troops on South Vietnamese positions

guerrilla war — a type of war fought with fast, hit-and-run attacks

Gulf of Tonkin Resolution — 1963 act of Congress giving President Johnson more power to fight in Vietnam

Hanoi — capital of North Vietnam during the Vietnam War; today it is the capital of Vietnam

hippies — young people who rejected the ways of older Americans in the 1960s

Ho Chi Minh — leader of North Vietnam during the Vietnam War

Hue — historic city heavily damaged during the Tet Offensive

Ia Drang Valley — valley in central Vietnam, site of U.S. victory in 1965

inflation — when prices go up quickly

Khe Sahn — remote Vietnam area, site of Marine base during Vietnam War

Khmer Rouge — rulers of Cambodia from 1975 to 1979

Laos — southeastern Asian country on western border of Vietnam; it was invaded during the Vietnam War

napalm — a weapon made from gasoline jelly

Ngo Dinh Diem — president of South Vietnam from 1955 to 1963

Nguyen Van Thieu — president of South Vietnam from 1967 to 1975

peaceniks — disrespectful term for people who opposed the Vietnam War

quagmire — a swamp that is hard to walk through; a term used to describe the Vietnam War

racist — being unfair or hostile to people of other races

Saigon — capital of South Vietnam during the Vietnam war; now called Ho Chi Minh City

search and destroy — mission in which soldiers would look for enemy troops or supplies and try to capture or kill them

Tet — the Vietnamese new year

Tet Offensive — major attack launched by NLF and NVA forces in January 1968

Viet Cong — disrespectful term for National Liberation Front (or NLF) forces

Viet Minh — group founded by Ho Chi Minh to fight for Vietnamese independence

war of attrition — a war in which one side simply tries to kill as many of the enemy as possible instead of capturing land

Index